HELEN HALL LIBRARY
City of League City
100 West Walker
League City, TX 77573-3899

DISCARD

D0744238

Jan 17

Meet the
SAN FRANCISCO
49ERS

BY
ZACK BURGESS

HELEN HALL LIBRARY
100 Walker St
League City, TX 77573
[DISCARD]

NORWOOD HOUSE 🏠 PRESS

CHICAGO, ILLINOIS

NORWOOD HOUSE 🏠 PRESS

P.O. Box 316598 • Chicago, Illinois 60631
For more information about Norwood House Press please visit our website at
www.norwoodhousepress.com or call 866-565-2900.

Photo Credits:
All photos courtesy of Associated Press, except for the following: Black Book Archives (6, 7, 18, 22, 23), Topps, Inc. (10 both, 11 top), McDonald's Corp. (11 middle), Donruss/Leaf–Panini America (11 bottom).

Cover Photo: Ric Tapia/Associated Press

The football memorabilia photographed for this book is part of the authors' collection. The collectibles used for artistic background purposes in this series were manufactured by many different card companies— including Bowman, Donruss, Fleer, Leaf, O-Pee-Chee, Pacific, Panini America, Philadelphia Chewing Gum, Pinnacle, Pro Line, Pro Set, Score, Topps, and Upper Deck—as well as several food brands, including Crane's, Hostess, Kellogg's, McDonald's and Post.

Designer: Ron Jaffe
Series Editors: Mike Kennedy and Mark Stewart
Project Management: Black Book Partners, LLC.
Editorial Production: Lisa Walsh

LIBRARY OF CONGRESS CATALOGING-IN-PUBLICATION DATA
Names: Burgess, Zack.
Title: Meet the San Francisco 49ers / by Zack Burgess.
Other titles: Meet the San Francisco Forty-niners
Description: Chicago, Illinois : Norwood House Press, [2016] | Series: Big
    picture sports | Includes bibliographical references and index. |
    Audience: Grades: K to Grade 3.
Identifiers: LCCN 2015023491| ISBN 9781599537221 (Library Edition : alk.
    paper) | ISBN 9781603578257 (eBook)
Subjects: LCSH: San Francisco 49ers (Football team)--Miscellanea--Juvenile
    literature.
Classification: LCC GV956.S3 B87 2016 | DDC 796.332/640979461--dc23
LC record available at http://lccn.loc.gov/2015023491

© 2017 by Norwood House Press. All rights reserved.
No part of this book may be reproduced without written permission from the publisher.
The San Francisco 49ers is a registered trademark of San Francisco Forty Niners, Ltd.
This publication is not affiliated with the San Francisco 49ers, San Francisco Forty Niners, Ltd.,
The National Football League, or The National Football League Players Association.

288N—072016
Manufactured in the United States of America in North Mankato, Minnesota

CONTENTS

Words in **bold type** are defined on page 24.

The 49ers
have great
team spirit.

CALL ME A 49ER

In the National Football League (NFL), teams copy one another all the time. The San Francisco 49ers are different. They have always loved new ideas. The 49ers are like the gold miners of 1849. They find special players that other teams overlook. The "'Niners" are willing to risk everything to discover new ways to win.

The 49ers played their first season in 1946. Over the years, they became known for winning games in exciting and unexpected ways. In the 1980s, the 49ers were one of the best teams in the NFL. They relied on stars such as **Dwight Clark** and Joe Montana.

MERTON HANKS FS

SAN FRANCISCO 49ERS

Amp Lee
Tailback

6

CK HARDMAN

Joe Montana was known as "The Comeback Kid."

7

There are no bad seats at a 49ers home game.

BEST SEAT IN THE HOUSE

For many years, the 49ers' home field was in (or near) San Francisco. In 2014, the team moved to a stadium an hour away in Santa Clara. Fans like it a lot. Every seat has an excellent view of the field.

DWIGHT CLARK
SAN FRANCISCO 49ERS · WR

TEAM OF THE DECADE 1990

FLEER TRADITION

JOHN TAYLOR

SHOE BOX

The trading cards on these pages show some of the best 49ers ever.

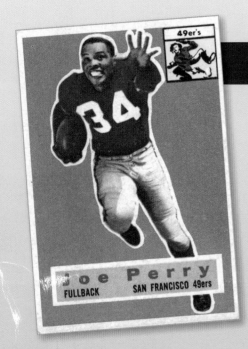

JOE PERRY

RUNNING BACK · 1948–1960 AND 1963

Joe "The Jet" was the fastest runner in the NFL. He learned good footwork and balance playing soccer as a boy.

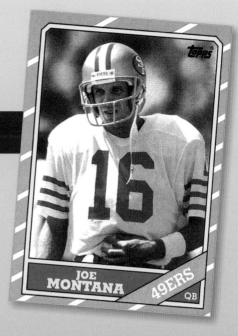

JOE MONTANA

QUARTERBACK · 1979–1992

Joe looked for a weakness in every team he faced. He gave the 49ers a chance to win every game they played.

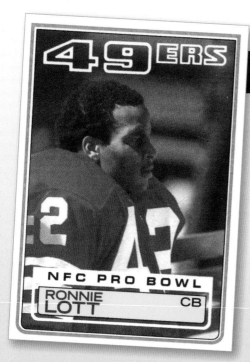

RONNIE LOTT

SAFETY · 1981–1990

Opponents had to know where Ronnie was at all times. He was one of football's hardest tacklers.

JERRY RICE

RECEIVER · 1985–2000

Jerry was one of the best pass-catchers in the NFL. He was voted into the **Hall of Fame** in 2010.

PATRICK WILLIS

LINEBACKER · 2007–2014

It often took two players to block Patrick. He was voted **All-Pro** five times.

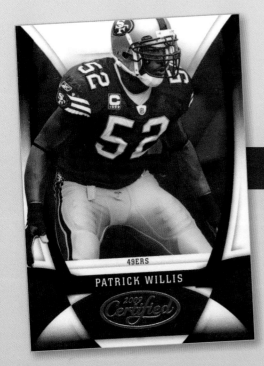

THE BIG PICTURE

Look at the two photos on page 13. Both appear to be the same. But they are not. There are three differences. Can you spot them?

Answers on page 23.

13

Frank Gore was a star running back. Two of these facts about him are **TRUE**. One is **FALSE**. Do you know which is which?

1 Frank made the **Pro Bowl** five times with the 49ers.

2 Frank once caught a touchdown pass with his feet.

3 Frank ran for more than 1,000 yards four seasons in a row. And he did it twice!

Answer on page 23.

Frank Gore breaks into the open.

A young 49ers fan gets a big surprise.

Go 49ers, Go!

At the team's old stadium, the weather could change suddenly. The 49ers started blowing a foghorn as a joke in the 1990s. Today, the team picks a fan to blow the foghorn at each game. It is one of the greatest honors a 49ers fan can have.

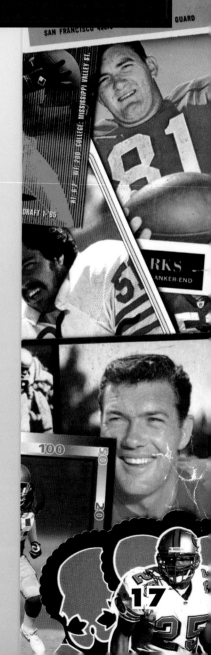

ON THE MAP

Here is a look at where five 49ers were born, along with a fun fact about each.

 STEVE YOUNG · SALT LAKE CITY, UTAH
Steve was the NFL's Most Valuable Player in 1992 and 1994.

 ROGER CRAIG · DAVENPORT, IOWA
Roger was the first player to gain 1,000 yards rushing and receiving in the same season.

 TERRELL OWENS · ALEXANDER CITY, ALABAMA
Terrell caught 100 passes and scored 13 touchdowns in 2002.

 BRUCE TAYLOR · PERTH AMBOY, NEW JERSEY
Bruce had 18 **interceptions** in seven seasons with the 49ers.

 LEO NOMELLINI · LUCCA, ITALY
In 14 seasons with the 49ers, Leo never missed a game.

NORTH

WEST · EAST

SOUTH

1

2

3

4

The 49ers' home city is San Francisco, California.

SAN FRANCISCO FORTY NINERS

SAN FRANCISCO FORTY NINERS

5

WORLD MAP

HOME AND AWAY

Aaron Lynch wears the 49ers' home uniform

Football teams wear different uniforms for home and away games. The main colors of the 49ers are red and gold. During the 1940s and 1950s, the team wore red and silver.

NaVorro Bowman wears the 49ers' away uniform.

The 49ers have gold helmets. They are a favorite of the fans. Each side of the helmet shows the letters *SF*. They stand for San Francisco.

WE WON!

The 49ers captured their first NFL championship in 1981. Over the next 13 seasons, they won the Super Bowl four more times. Three coaches led the team to the big game. They are **Bill Walsh**, George Seifert, and Jim Harbaugh.

RECORD BOOK

These 49ers set team records.

PASSING YARDS		RECORD
Season:	Jeff Garcia (2000)	4,278
Career:	Joe Montana	35,124

TOUCHDOWN CATCHES		RECORD
Season:	**Jerry Rice** (1987)	22
Career:	Jerry Rice	176

FIELD GOALS		RECORD
Season:	David Akers (2011)	44
Career:	Ray Wersching	190

ANSWERS FOR THE BIG PICTURE
#77 changed to #87, the goal posts changed to blue, and the red stadium display changed to orange.

ANSWER FOR TRUE AND FALSE
#2 is false. Frank never caught a touchdown pass with his feet.

FOOTBALL WORDS

INDEX

All-Pro
An honor given to the best NFL player at each position.

Hall of Fame
The museum in Canton, Ohio, where football's greatest players are honored.

Interceptions
Passes caught by a defensive player.

Pro Bowl
The NFL's annual all-star game.

ABOUT THE AUTHOR

Zack Burgess has been writing about sports for more than 20 years. He has lived all over the country and interviewed lots of All-Pro football players, including Brett Favre, Eddie George, Jerome Bettis, Shannon Sharpe, and Rich Gannon. Zack was the first African American beat writer to cover Major League Baseball when he worked for the *Kansas City Star*.

ABOUT THE 49ERS

Learn more at these websites:

www.49ers.com • www.profootballhof.com

www.teamspiritextras.com/Overtime/html/49ers.html

24

HELEN HALL LIBRARY
City of League City
100 West Walker
League City, TX 77573-3899